Pintxos

Delicious & Authentic Recipes

susaeta

Contents

Bitesize cuisine from San Sebastian

The custom of having an appetiser before a meal is common throughout the whole of Spain, going by a different name depending on the region. The tapa originated during the time of Alfonso X. The monarch suggested that wine should be accompanied with some solid food such as cold cuts, cheese or a slice of ham, which could double up as a means to cover the jug and prevent dirt or other objects from falling in.

The tapa is now one of the most widely known "inventions" both in Spain and across the world. Many can claim to have tried tapas such as fried morcilla, tripe, sweetbreads, Spanish omelette or grilled pig's ear.

The word pintxo was more recently coined and is one of the great discoveries of the Basque Country. The pintxo originated in the suburbs of San Sebastian and can be described as an extraordinary branch of the tapa concept, displaying an array of contrasting aromas, colours and wonderful flavours.

San Sebastian offers an extremely varied selection of pintxos to anyone ready to explore its neighbourhoods and the myriad of bars and restaurants.

Go and savour a range of delicious appetisers before your main meal; take a typical tasting route or a "pintxo crawl".

Decoration techniques

STEP BY STEP

Decoration is one of the most important factors to consider when you present pintxos you have made. A good combination of textures and flavours will make the tapas more attractive and tasty-looking.

However, decoration should not present any major challenges due to the size of pintxos and the fact that there are actually few possible combinations of ingredients.

The key to producing pintxos as attractive as those in this book is simply to make sure you always choose fresh, good quality ingredients and that you follow the step-by-step instructions.

In this section we show you two types of decoration: one that teaches you how to enhance a dish itself, and another with the instructions you need to make a table decoration.

A simple and attractive way of decorating a dish is to make a little basket using a lemon.

If you want to decorate the table, it is best to opt for something more spectacular, such as the Gilda pintxo decoration shown on the next page or the pickled anchovies wheel here.

Pickled anchovies wheel

1. The ingredients you need to make the pickled anchovies wheel are: olives, fresh anchovies marinated in vinegar and cherry tomatoes.
2. To make, skewer the three ingredients with a cocktail stick or toothpick and make as many pintxos as you want.
3. Once you have made all the pintxos, place them on a platter or large plate, making sure the pintxos stay in the same position.
4. The next ring of pintxos can be put on top of these or else towards the centre of the plate, creating as many circles as you like.

Gilda

1. Place an olive, a pickled green chilli, a slice of red piquillo pepper, a small pickled onion and a pickled gherkin on a plate.
2. Then skewer the ingredients with a kebab stick following the order in Step 1.
3. Once you have skewered all the ingredients, you have Gilda pintxo.
4. For an even more spectacular effect, skewer the pintxos into a lemon.

Lemon basket

1. Cut one end of the lemon off with a sharp knife. On the top end of the lemon, make two cuts to a little more than half way down.
2. From the end of each cut, make small, even cuts, forming a zigzag.
3. Discard the unused part from the centre.
4. There you have your lemon basket.

Pintxos with fish

Biscay white tuna
with onions

Bread
Pickled Biscay white tuna
Onion
Mayonnaise
Vinegar
Capers
Anchovies in olive oil

PREPARATION

1. Break the pickled tuna into flakes.
2. Slice the onion very finely.
3. Mix both ingredients together with the mayonnaise and add a dash of vinegar as well as the capers.
4. Spread the mixture over a slice of bread and garnish with an anchovy.

Biscay white tuna with onions

Deep fried anchovies
with piquillo peppers

Bread

Anchovies

Salt

Piquillo peppers

Flour

Egg

Oil

PREPARATION

1. Clean the anchovies and remove the bones.
2. Wash the peppers and roast in the oven until the skins come off easily. Once they have cooled, peel off the skin and set to one side. You could also use tinned peppers instead.
3. Put an anchovy on top of a pepper and cover with another anchovy.
4. Add salt and then dip in flour and egg.
5. Pour plenty of olive oil into a frying pan and when hot, add the coated anchovies.
6. Remove when golden coloured.
7. Cut the bread into even-sized slices, put the battered anchovies on the bread and serve the pintxos hot.

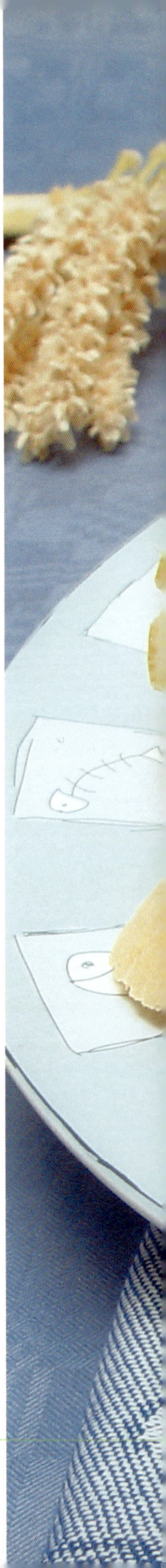

Prawns *a la gabardina*

Prawns

Sparkling water

Yeast

Salt

Flour

PREPARATION

1. Pour sparkling water into a bowl and add yeast, salt and flour. Stir together until it becomes a paste.
2. Then add the prawns to the mixture.
3. Fry the prawns in very hot olive oil.
4. Serve hot.

Salt cod brandade

Bread
Cod
Garlic
Chilli
Olive oil
Milk

PREPARATION

1. Desalt the cod the day before, changing the water repeatedly.
2. Chop 4 cloves of garlic and one chilli.
3. Heat the olive oil in a pan and fry the garlic and chilli.
4. Remove from the pan and fry the cod slowly in the same oil.
5. Once the cod is done, peel it, remove the bones and crumble into bits.
6. Then blend the cod together with the oil, garlic and chilli.
7. Once you have a smooth texture, gradually add the milk, beating the cod into it until you get a brandade of a consistent texture.
8. Cut the bread into slices and spread the mixture on top.
9. Finally, put the pintxos in the oven and bake.

Cod fillets

Fresh cod fillets

Flour

Egg

Salt

PREPARATION

1. Season the cod fillets and dip them in flour and egg.
2. Heat up plenty of olive oil in a frying pan. Once the oil is hot, fry the fillets until they turn golden brown.
3. Arrange the cod fillets on individual plates. You may garnish the dishes with orange slices you have sculpted beforehand.

Cod fillets

Salmon rolls

with cheese

Breadsticks
Smoked salmon
Slices of cheese
Tomato
1 piquillo pepper

PREPARATION

1. Wash the tomato and cut into slices.
2. Slice the salmon and the cheese into even rectangles.
3. Place the salmon and cheese on top of each other and make into a roll.
4. Place a slice of tomato on top of two breadsticks. Place the salmon and cheese roll on top of this.
5. Finally decorate the roll with a mini slice of cheese and piquillo pepper.

Salmon rolls with cheese

Crab tartlets

Pastry cases

Boiled spider crab

Endives

Mayonnaise

Piquillo pepper

PREPARATION

1. Boil the crab for 15 minutes per approximately one kilo of crab.
2. Once cooked, break the flesh into flakes.
3. Wash the endive leaves thoroughly to remove the bitter taste and dry them. Save some whole leaves for garnish and slice the rest into thin strips.
4. Mix the flaked crab with the mayonnaise and endive leaves.
5. Fill the pastry cases with the mixture and garnish with the whole leaves and a slice of piquillo pepper.

Fresh anchovies

Vinegar

Water

Garlic

Olive oil

Parsley

Presentation:

Pitted olives

Cherry tomatoes

Pickled anchovies

PREPARATION

1. Clean the anchovies, remove the bones and then wash them.
2. Leave the anchovies in a bowl with cold water for about eight hours. Keep changing the water until they are free of blood.
3. Drain the water off, add a handful of salt and cover with vinegar. Let them stand for another eight hours.
4. Remove the vinegar, rinse with cold water and drain.
5. Then dress the anchovies with a spurt of olive oil, a little salt, a dash of vinegar, finely chopped garlic and parsley.
6. Make the skewers as shown on page 8.

Anchovies

with black olive pâté

Bread

Pickled anchovies

Black olives

Olive oil

Garlic

PREPARATION

1. First, make some pickled anchovies as shown in the recipe on the previous page.
2. Cut the bread into slices and cover with two anchovies.
3. Remove the stones from the olives and, using a mixer, blend them with the garlic and a drizzle of olive oil until smooth.
4. Spread the paste over the anchovies and garnish with a bit of green pepper.

Anchovies with black olive pâté

Salmon with tuna

and Marie Rose sauce

- Sliced bread
- Canned Biscay white tuna
- Marie Rose sauce
- Smoked salmon
- Onion
- Cherry tomatoes

PREPARATION

1. Remove the crusts from the bread and slice into the size you want.
2. Crumble the tuna and mix it in with the Marie Rose sauce to make a creamy paste.
3. Spread a layer of Marie Rose sauce onto a slice of bread, put the tuna mix on top, place another slice of bread over this and then spread with Marie Rose sauce again.
4. Then put a slice of salmon the same size as the bread on the top.
5. Garnish with the chopped onion strips and cherry tomatoes.

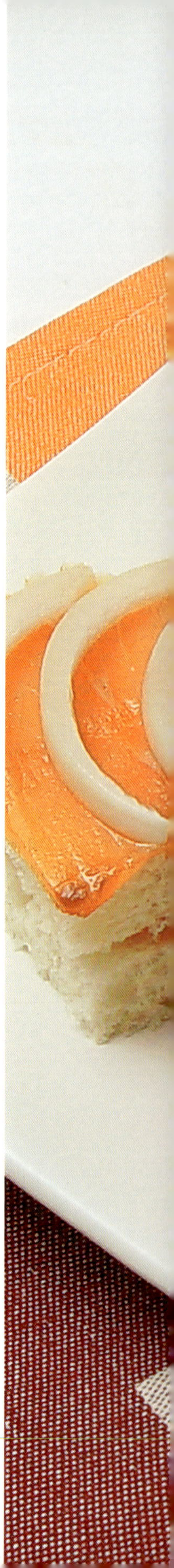

Pintxos with egg

Egg on anchovy
with onion and parsley

Bread

Anchovies

Egg

Onion

Parsley

Mayonnaise

PREPARATION

1. Use a slice of bread as a base.
2. Place two anchovies on the bread lengthwise.
3. Hard boil the egg, cut into quarters and then cut the quarters in half.
4. Place one of the egg triangles at one end of the bread and cover with a little mayonnaise.
5. Chop the onion finely and mix with some chopped parsley. Spread this over the other end of the bread.

Egg on anchovy with onion and parsley

Quail egg tarts
with vegetables

Pastry cases
Olive oil
Onion
Courgette
Piquillo pepper
Cooked prawns
Quail eggs

PREPARATION

1. Use a pastry case as a base.
2. Chop the onion and let it soften slowly in a frying pan with a little olive oil.
3. Add the very finely chopped courgette and fry it slowly together with the onion.
4. Tip the fried onion and courgette into a pastry case.
5. Roast the pepper in the oven until the skin comes off easily or alternatively use canned peppers. Garnish with finely chopped pepper.
6. Place a cooked prawn on top of the pepper.
7. Finally, fry the eggs and put one on top of each tartlet.

Quail egg tarts with vegetables

Fried quail eggs
with chorizo

Bread
Olive oil
Quail eggs
Piquillo peppers
Spicy chorizo

PREPARATION

1. Cut bread into even sized slices.
2. Fry the eggs in a pan in hot olive oil.
3. Cut the chorizo into thin slices and fry in the same oil.
4. Place a slice of piquillo pepper on each slice of bread, a fried egg over that and then the slices of chorizo on top.
5. Serve hot.

Bread
Piquillo peppers
Anchovies in oil
Eggs
Mayonnaise
Marie Rose sauce

Eggs with piquillo peppers
and anchovies in two sauces

PREPARATION

1. Cut slices of bread and place them on a platter.
2. If using raw pepper, roast in the oven until the skin peels off easily. Remove skin once cool, cut off a strip and place on the bread.
3. Put two anchovies over the pepper.
4. Boil the eggs and cut them into slices. Put a slice of egg on the anchovies.
5. Garnish with both sauces, putting a little of each on the egg without mixing them.

Fried quail eggs
with Jabugo ham

Bread

Jabugo ham

Olive oil

Quail eggs

PREPARATION

1. Cut the bread into thick, even slices.
2. Place a slice of Jabugo ham on each slice of bread.
3. In a pan, heat the olive oil and fry the eggs without burning them.
4. Put the fried egg on top of the ham and decorate to your liking.

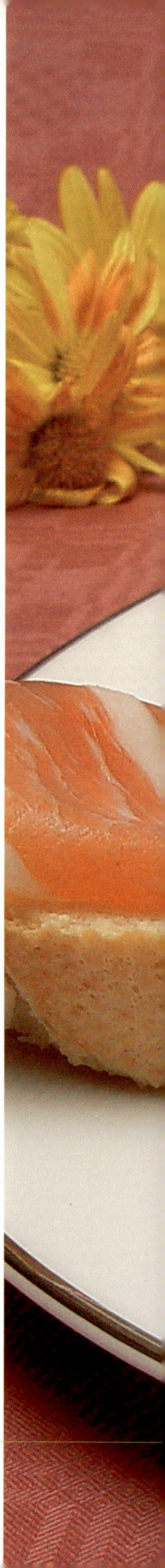

Fried quail eggs with Jabugo ham

Eggs with Serrano ham,

salmon and prawn

Toasted bread

Serrano ham

Smoked salmon

Eggs

Mayonnaise

Prawns

PREPARATION

1. Place a slice of Serrano ham on the slice of bread.
2. Put a slice of smoked salmon on top of the Serrano ham.
3. In a saucepan, boil the eggs for about 10 minutes until they are hard.
4. Peel off the shell, cut into slices and arrange them over the salmon. Add a dab of mayonnaise.
5. Cook the prawns for a few minutes then peel them.
6. Finally, skewer the prawn with a cocktail stick and then pierce it through the egg too.

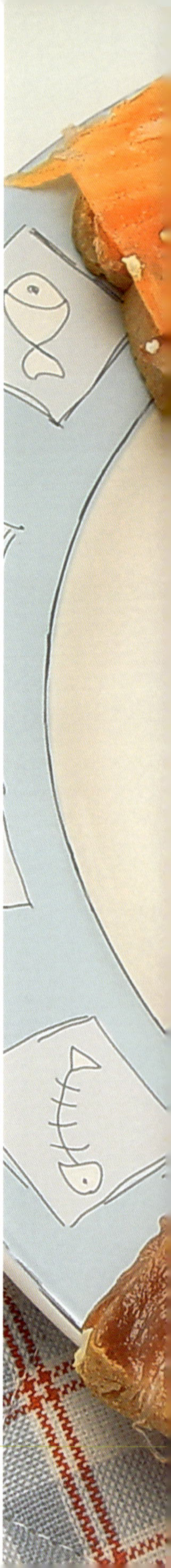

Eggs with Serrano ham, salmon and prawn

Eggs with Biscay tuna

Bread

Eggs

Biscay white tuna

Mayonnaise

Stuffed olives

Piquillo peppers

PREPARATION

1. Boil the eggs for about 10 minutes until hard.
2. Take off the shell, cut each egg in half and place on a plate.
3. Put a piece of the tuna on each half.
4. Add a little mayonnaise to the tuna.
5. Place an olive on each egg.
6. Roast the pepper in the oven until the skin comes off easily. Leave to cool, remove the skin and cut into thin strips. If you are using tinned peppers, drain and cut into very thin strips.
7. Place a strip of pepper around the olive for garnish; accompany each pintxo with a slice of bread.

Eggs

Mayonnaise

Prawns

Manzanilla olives

Eggs with mayonnaise
and prawns

PREPARATION

1. Boil the eggs and cut them in half.
2. Arrange on a platter and put a little mayonnaise on each egg half to decorate.
3. Cook the prawns in plenty of salted water. Once they are cool remove the shell and heads and put a prawn on each egg.
4. Use olives to garnish; if you wish you can skewer them onto the prawn with a cocktail stick.

Quail egg tarts
with caviar and anchovies

Pastry cases
Anchovies
Quail eggs
Mayonnaise
Caviar

PREPARATION

1. Use the pastry cases as a base.
2. Cut the anchovies into strips and place on the bottom of each pastry case.
3. Boil the eggs for a few minutes until hard.
4. Peel off the shell, cut the eggs in half and place them on the anchovies.
5. Put two dabs of mayonnaise to the sides of the eggs and a little caviar on top.

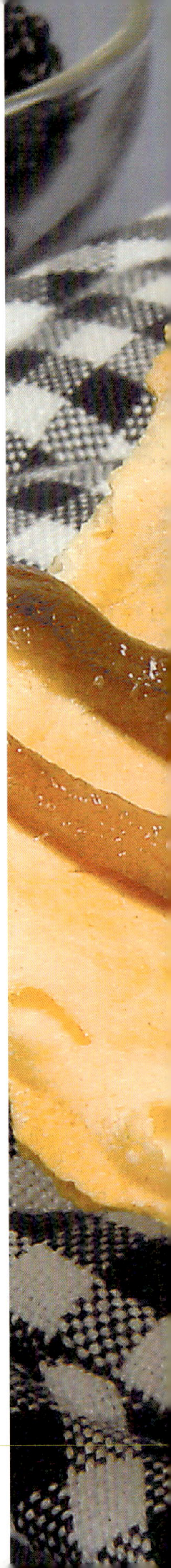

Eggs with piquillo peppers

and lettuce

Bread

Lettuce

Eggs

Piquillo peppers

Mayonnaise

Anchovies

PREPARATION

1. Cut off a slice of bread and use as a base for the pintxo.
2. Wash the lettuce in plenty of cold water for a few minutes and drain. Place a lettuce leaf on each slice.
3. Boil the eggs, peel and cut in half. Cut a little piece off the end of each half, to use as a lid. Put the egg on the lettuce.
4. Roast the red pepper in the oven until the skin comes off easily.
5. Once cool, peel and cut off a slice to place on each egg. You can also use tinned peppers.
6. Place the egg lid on top.
7. Decorate with a little mayonnaise.
8. Put an anchovy on the mayonnaise and pierce with a cocktail stick to hold in place.

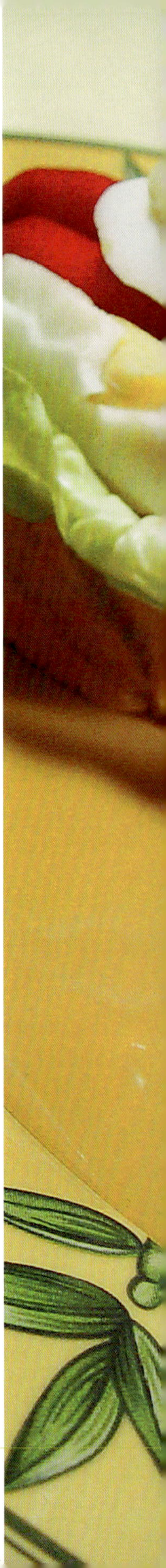

Eggs with piquillo peppers and lettuce

Pintxos with vegetables

Green asparagus
with ham

Green asparagus
Piquillo pepper
Jabugo ham
Savoury crackers

PREPARATION

1. Wash the asparagus and use only the tips.
2. Boil the asparagus in lightly salted water until they are slightly soft and leave to cool.
3. Place a piece of piquillo pepper on the cracker, then wrap the Jabugo ham around the tip of the asparagus and place on the pepper.
4. You may want to decorate the dish with half a lemon and a slice of rolled pepper.

Green asparagus with ham

Piquillo and green peppers

Bread

Green peppers

Piquillo peppers

Olive oil

Crab meat

Mayonnaise

Egg

Lemon

PREPARATION

1. Wash the green peppers, cut off the top and remove the seeds from the inside.
2. In a frying pan, heat the oil, fry the peppers over a medium heat until they are soft and put to one side.
3. Drain the piquillo peppers if using tinned ones. If using fresh peppers, roast them in the oven until the skin comes off easily. Peel off the skin once cold and set aside.
4. Mix the crab meat and mayonnaise together well.
5. Stuff the peppers with the mix.
6. Place the peppers on the bread slices and place them on a dish, alternating between red and green.
7. Boil the egg in a saucepan for approximately 10 minutes. Peel off the shell and cut into small triangles.
8. Garnish the dish with an egg placed on a lemon basket.

Piquillo and green peppers

Vegetable brochette

with prawns

Mushrooms
Prawns
Green 'Guernica' peppers
Hot red peppers
Coarse salt
Garlic
Parsley
Olive oil
Vinegar

PREPARATION

1. Stick a skewer through a mushroom, a green pepper, a prawn, a hot red pepper, another mushroom and finally another prawn.
2. Cook the skewers on the grill. Once they are done, sprinkle over some coarse salt.
3. If you would like a sauce to accompany the brochette, finely chop some garlic and parsley, add the vinegar and beat with a whisk while slowly adding the olive oil.

Morcilla

Green cabbage

Cabbage cones
with morcilla

PREPARATION

1. Select different types of blood sausage, preferably the Spanish variety called morcilla. Cook to get the fat out.
2. Remove the skin once cold and mix the meats together.
3. Boil the green cabbage leaves in a saucepan, until soft.
4. Place the blood sausage meat in the cabbage leaves and serve hot.

Piquillo pepper mousse

Vol-au-vent cases
Fresh piquillo peppers
Garlic
Salt
Sugar
Olive oil
Onion
Cream
Eggs
Pepper
Caviar

PREPARATION

1. Wash the peppers, add salt, garlic and sugar and roast for a few minutes until the skin comes off easily.
2. Heat the oil in a frying pan and add the finely chopped onion.
3. Once the onions are nice and soft, add the peppers and season with some pepper.
4. Mix everything in a blender and then push it through a conical strainer to produce a light purée.
5. In a bowl, beat the eggs and cream, add the puréed peppers and cook in a bain-marie in the oven for about 1 hour.
6. Fill the vol-au-vent shells with the cooked mixture and decorate with a little caviar.

Piquillo pepper mousse

Vegetable brochette

Artichokes
White asparagus
Eggs
Anchovies
Olive oil
Vinegar
Onion
Piquillo peppers
Salt

PREPARATION

1. If using fresh artichokes you will need to boil them beforehand. You can also use the pre-prepared, canned variety.
2. Boil the eggs in plenty of water for 10 minutes.
3. Skewer one half of an artichoke.
4. Then skewer a piece of asparagus.
5. Add another artichoke.
6. Finally add a piece of hard-boiled egg and an anchovy to the skewer.
7. In a bowl, mix the finely chopped onion, piquillo pepper cut into small pieces, vinegar, salt and olive oil and pour it over the brochette.

Vegetable brochette

Mushroom *txapela*

Mushrooms
Salt
Olive oil
White pepper
Garlic
Chopped Serrano ham
Milk
Jabugo ham
Flour
Egg
Breadcrumbs

PREPARATION

1. Clean the mushrooms, remove the stalks and season half of the *txapelas* (caps) with a little salt, pepper and a few drops of olive oil.
2. Peel and chop a garlic clove, then sprinkle on top.
3. Chop a few slices of ham and add to the mushrooms.
4. Put a little olive oil in a saucepan. Heat it gently without letting it burn. When it is nice and hot, add a few tablespoons of flour and let it brown a little. Turn down the heat and add a little milk, stirring continuously until you have a thick béchamel sauce. Season to taste.
5. Pour some of the béchamel sauce over the ham.
6. Use the other half of the *txapelas* as a lid to cover the stuffed ones and push down a little.
7. Coat in flour, egg and breadcrumbs.
8. Fry them in plenty of hot olive oil.
9. Decorate the pintxo with a little ham shaped like a flower.

Pickled Biscay tuna

Onion

Mayonnaise

Vinegar

Tartare sauce

Piquillo peppers from Mendavia

Salt

Stuffed piquillo peppers

PREPARATION

1. Crumble the tuna into flakes and finely chop the onion.
2. Mix both ingredients together with a little mayonnaise.
3. Add a little vinegar and tartare sauce to the mixture. Put to one side.
4. Drain the piquillo peppers if you are using tinned ones. If using fresh peppers, roast in the oven beforehand until the skin peels off easily.
5. Fill them with the mixture and season to taste with a little salt.

Stuffed mushrooms

Mushrooms
Onion
Red Peppers
Green peppers
Veal, turkey or fish
Béchamel sauce
Breadcrumbs
Olive oil

PREPARATION

1. Cut the stalks off the mushrooms
2. Finely chop the onion and green and red peppers.
3. Cut the veal into small pieces.
4. Cook the mushroom stalks on a low heat with the chopped vegetables and veal. You could also use turkey or fish.
5. Once you have prepared this delicious mix, set to one side to fill the mushroom hats with later.
6. Prepare a béchamel sauce (see p. 58, step 4).
7. Once you have stuffed the mushrooms, dip them in the béchamel and then coat in breadcrumbs.
8. Fry in plenty of hot olive oil and serve piping hot.

Stuffed mushrooms

Gilda

Large olives
Pickled green chillies
Piquillo peppers
Pickled onions
Pickled gherkins

PREPARATION

1. If using fresh peppers, roast for a few minutes in the oven, turning them over occasionally. When cool, peel off the skin. You can also use canned peppers.
2. Using a cocktail stick, gently skewer an olive, a chilli, a rolled-up piquillo pepper, a pickled onion and finally the gherkin.
3. You can serve the pintxo directly on a plate or, if you want to use it as a table decoration, stick several of them into a lemon.

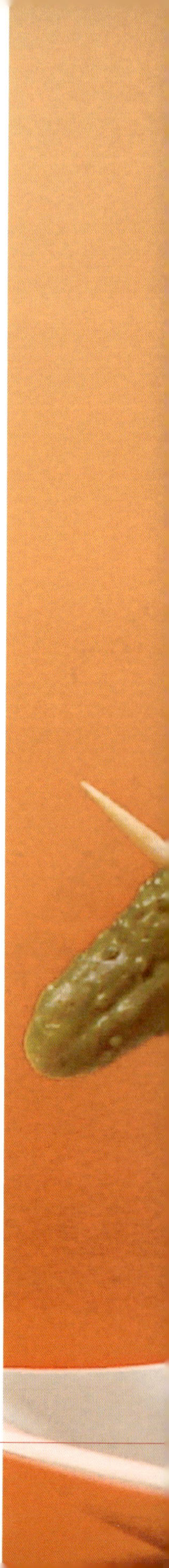

Gilda

Assorted
pintxos

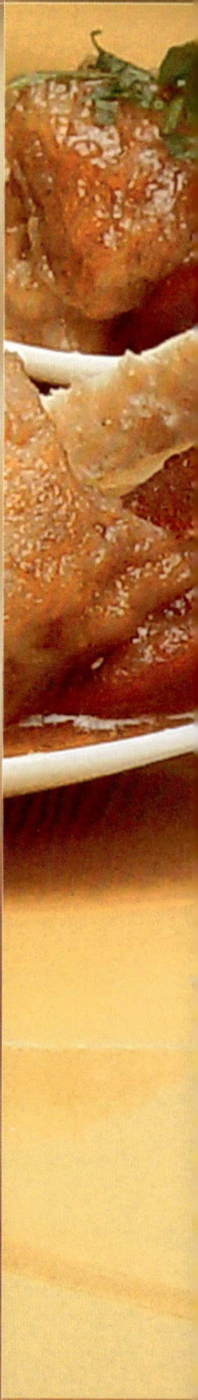

Roquefort

with anchovies and palm hearts

- Bread
- Anchovies
- Roquefort cheese
- Palm hearts
- Piquillo pepper
- Parsley

PREPARATION

1. Cut up some slices of baguette or you can use melba toast.
2. Place two anchovies on each slice.
3. Put a slice of Roquefort on top of the anchovies, at one end of the bread.
4. Drain the palm hearts, cut diagonally and arrange them on the other end of the bread.
5. Garnish with piquillo pepper and parsley. You can also cut a few pieces of palm heart lengthwise to use as garnish.

Roquefort with anchovies and palm hearts

White asparagus

with white tuna and mayonnaise

Bread

Mayonnaise

White asparagus from a jar

Biscay white tuna

Capers

PREPARATION

1. Cut up some slices of bread or you can use melba toast.
2. Spread each slice of bread with some mayonnaise.
3. Drain the asparagus well to make sure you remove any excess liquid.
4. Place 2 pieces of asparagus on each slice of bread.
5. Drain the tuna and cut it into cubes. Place the cubes along the lengths of asparagus.
6. Place the capers along the asparagus, between the tuna cubes.
7. If you wish, you can garnish the plate with sculpted orange slices.

White asparagus with white tuna and mayonnaise

Basque-style tripe

Bread
Beef Tripe
Lemon
Vinegar
Onion
Carrots
Parsley
Bay leaves
Whole peppercorns
Salt

PREPARATION

1. Wash and scrape the tripe with great care before boiling them, changing the water several times.
2. Then put them in a bowl with vinegar, salt and chopped lemon until they turn white.
3. It is a good idea to boil the tripe for several hours the day before.
4. Cut the tripe into small pieces and put in a saucepan with cold water.
5. Boil for 5 minutes, remove the water, refill with fresh water and add the remaining ingredients. Bring to the boil and then leave to simmer for 4 hours.
6. Once you have prepared the tripe, put a small amount on a slice of bread and serve hot.

Roquefort cheese

Single cream

Piquillo pepper

Roquefort delight

PREPARATION

1. Cut the Roquefort into chunks and mix with the cream.
2. If using a fresh red pepper, roast for a few minutes until the skin comes off easily. If canned, drain to remove excess liquid.
3. Chop the peppers into small pieces.
4. Place a little of the Roquefort sauce on ceramic serving spoons and garnish with a piece of pepper.
5. If you wish, you can also spread the Roquefort sauce on toast and garnish with a few walnuts.

Green chicken

Bread

Chicken Breasts

Lettuce

Onion

Mayonnaise

PREPARATION

1. Cut up the chicken breasts and fry in olive oil.
2. Break the fried chicken into pieces and set to one side.
3. Wash the lettuce thoroughly in cold water. Chop up and spin off the excess water.
4. Prepare some mayonnaise using egg, lemon, vinegar and salt and add the finely chopped onion.
5. Mix together and place on a slice of bread.

Green chicken

Chicken salad

tartlets

Pastry cases

Chicken

Lettuce

Sweetcorn

Mayonnaise

PREPARATION

1. Cook the chicken in a saucepan for a few minutes.
2. Wash the lettuce carefully and spin to remove excess water.
3. Crumble the chicken into bits and finely chop the lettuce.
4. Mix all the ingredients together with mayonnaise and add the sweetcorn.
5. Fill the pastry cases with the prepared mixture and garnish with a little sweetcorn.

Chicken salad tartlets

Liver pâté tartlets

with raisins

Pastry cases

Foie gras

Butter

Flaked raw almonds

Raisins

PREPARATION

1. In a bowl, mix the foie gras pâté with butter to make into a thicker paste.
2. Buy raw almond flakes.
3. In a hot frying pan, lightly toast the almonds being careful not to burn them.
4. Fill the pastry cases with the pâté mix, put some raisins on the top and add the toasted almonds.
5. If you wish, you can garnish the plate with a little orange basket with some maraschino cherries inside.

Cooked ham
Cheese
Mushrooms
Serrano ham
80 g butter
2 - 3 tablespoons flour
3/4 litre milk
Pepper
Salt
Lemon juice
Egg
Breadcrumbs

Cooked ham rolls

with mushrooms and ham

PREPARATION

1. Clean the mushrooms with a paper towel, chop into small pieces and sprinkle with lemon juice so they do not darken. Put to one side.
2. Finely chop the Serrano ham. Set to one side.
3. Heat a saucepan and add the butter. When it has melted, add the flour and sauté, stirring with a wooden spoon for a few minutes without allowing the flour to toast.
4. Keep stirring while pouring the milk in and taking care not to let lumps form. When the mixture has a thin consistency, season with salt, ground pepper and add the chopped mushrooms and ham. Simmer for 10 minutes, stirring continuously.
5. Place a slice of cheese on top of a slice of cooked ham. Coat the two slices with the béchamel sauce once it has cooled and then dip first in egg and then in breadcrumbs.
6. Fry in plenty of olive oil.
7. On top of each roll place a slice of mushroom and a small slice of rolled Serrano ham.

Garlic shoots omelette

1/2 kg potatoes

200 g wild garlic shoots

4 eggs

Salt

Bread

PREPARATION

1. Peel the potatoes and cut into slices. Fry in plenty of oil until soft. Drain off the oil and set aside.
2. Remove the outer leaves from the garlic shoots as well as the greener tips.
3. Carefully chop the garlic shoots and sauté in a frying pan with olive oil over a low heat.
4. Remove from the pan once done.
5. In a bowl, beat the eggs, mix with the sautéed garlic shoots and add salt.
6. Heat a little olive oil in a frying pan. Add the potatoes as well as the egg and sautéed garlic shoots mixture. Cook the omelette on a low heat. Don't cook for too long to ensure it has a slightly juicy consistency.
7. Finally, cut the omelette into little squares and place on the bread.

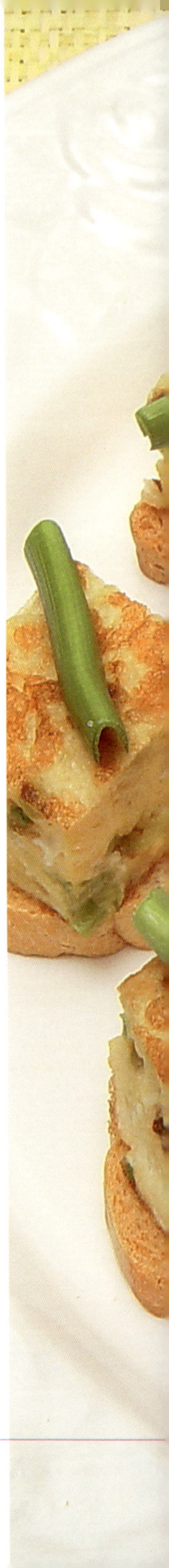

Garlic shoots omelette

Mini turkey escalopes
with mushrooms

Bread

Egg

Breadcrumbs

Turkey steaks

Green peppers

Oyster mushrooms

PREPARATION

1. Wash the peppers, cut off the stalks and remove the seeds from the inside.
2. Coat the turkey fillets in egg and then breadcrumbs. Fry them in plenty of olive oil together with the green peppers.
3. Peel the peppers once they have cooled.
4. Clean the mushrooms with a paper towel so they do not absorb water. Once they are clean, cook on the grill.
5. Place the green pepper on a slice of bread, then add the breaded turkey and on top of this the mushrooms.

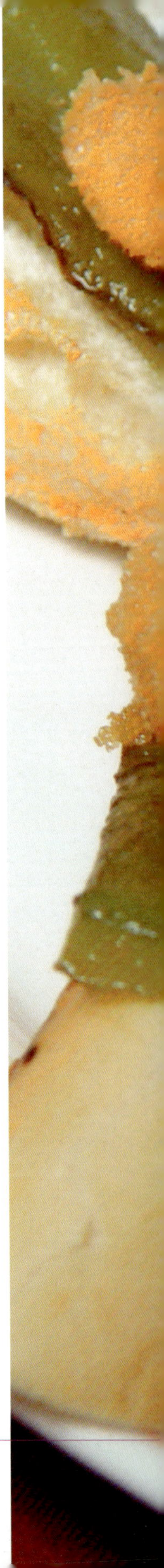

Mini turkey escalopes with mushrooms

Sweet pintxos

Caramelized pineapple

1 large pastry case
1/2 litre milk
3 egg yolks
2 tablespoons cornflour
75 g sugar
25 g butter
Zest of 1 lemon
Pineapples in syrup
Sugar for caramelizing

PREPARATION

1. Mix the egg yolks, sugar and cornflour in a small pan, gradually adding the milk which has previously been brought to the boil.
2. Then add the lemon zest, beat the mixture with a whisk and heat on the hob.
3. When it starts to boil, remove from the heat, add the butter and leave to cool.
4. Once you have made the custard mix, blend in a little bit of the pineapple syrup using a whisk and put the custard into the pastry case.
5. Cut the pineapple into equal sized pieces and place on top of the custard mix.
6. To decorate this pintxo, melt some sugar in a pan. Spread a little oil over a smooth surface and then pour the sugar over making the pattern of your choice.

Caramelized pineapple

Strawberries

with bread and chocolate

Toasted bread

Strawberries

Dark chocolate

White chocolate

PREPARATION

1. Wash the strawberries to remove any dirt and then dry them.
2. Melt the white and dark chocolate separately in a saucepan.
3. Dip the strawberries into the different kinds of melted chocolate and wait for the chocolate to set.
4. Finally, place the strawberries on top of the slices of toast.

Strawberries with bread and chocolate

Kiwi millefeuille

with boiled potato, pâté and raisins

Melba toast
Potato
Kiwi
Pâté
Raisins

PREPARATION

1. Use small slices of melba toast.
2. Boil the potatoes and leave to cool. Once cooled, peel off the skin, cut into slices about half a centimetre thick. Using a round mould the same size as the bread, cut them into shape.
3. Take a slab of pâté and use the mould to cut it into the same shape as the potatoes.
4. Peel the kiwi and cut into slices the same size as the potatoes and pâté.
5. Layer the potato, pâté, more potato and the kiwi over the melba toast.
6. Decorate with raisins.

Kiwi millefeuille with boiled potato, pâté and raisins

Sweet vol-au-vents

Vol-au-vent cases
1/2 litre milk
3 egg yolks
2 tablespoons cornflour
75 g sugar
25 g butter
Zest of 1 lemon
Instant coffee powder
Liquid chocolate

PREPARATION

1. Put the egg yolks, sugar and cornflour into a small pan, gradually adding the previously boiled milk.
2. Then add the lemon zest, beat the mixture with a whisk and heat.
3. When it starts to boil, remove from the heat, add the butter and leave to cool.
4. Once you have made the custard mix, use a whisk to whip in the instant coffee and liquid chocolate.
5. Fill the vol-au-vent cases with the custard mix and sprinkle some chocolate chips over them.

Sweet vol-au-vents

Scallop of red berries

Scallop-shaped pastry case
1/2 litre milk
3 egg yolks
3 tablespoons cornflour
75 g sugar
25 g butter
Zest of 1 lemon
Blackberries
Strawberries
Raspberries
Redcurrants

PREPARATION

1. Put the egg yolks, sugar and cornflour into a small pan, gradually stirring in the previously boiled milk.
2. Then add the lemon zest, beat the mixture with a whisk and heat.
3. When it starts to boil, remove from the heat, add the butter and leave to cool.
4. Once the custard mix is made, pour it into the pastry case.
5. Lastly, sprinkle the berries over the custard.

Scallop of red berries

Cheese and quince jelly
sandwich

Cured cheese

Quince jelly

PREPARATION

1. Cut the cheese into triangles with a cheese knife. If you do not have a cheese knife, you can heat a normal knife to cut the cheese more easily.
2. Cut the quince jelly into slices of the same size as the cheese.
3. Sandwich a triangle of quince jelly between two triangles of cheese.
4. Decorate by adding strips of quince jelly on the top of each sandwich.

Cheese and quince jelly sandwich

Production: Working Image & Design S.L.

Translation: Eleanor Pitt

Photography: Concha López

Design: Concha López y Laura García

Cover design: Sara Boix

Pre-press: Miguel Ángel San Andrés

Our gratitude to Jesus Vega for his contribution towards designing the recipes and the decoration. Our appreciation also to the shop Casa.

Campezo, 13 - 28022 Madrid
Tel.: 91 3009100 - Fax: 91 3009118
Impreso y encuadernado en España
www.susaeta.com

D.L.: M-4681-MMXV